WHEN RAP SPOKE STRAIGHT TO GOD

A POEM

ERICA DAWSON

WHEN RAP SPOKE STRAIGHT TO GOD

A POEM

 TIN HOUSE BOOKS / Portland, Oregon & Brooklyn, New York

Published by Tin House Books, Portland, Oregon, and Brooklyn, New York

Distributed by W. W. Norton & Company

Library of Congress Cataloging-in-Publication Data

Names: Dawson, Erica, 1979- author.
Title: When rap spoke straight to God / Erica Dawson.
Description: First U.S. edition. | Portland, OR : Tin House Books, 2018.
Identifiers: LCCN 2018021938| ISBN 9781947793033 (paperback) |
    ISBN 9781947793095 (ebook)
Classification: LCC PS3604.A9786 W48 2018 | DDC 811/.6—dc23
LC record available at https://lccn.loc.gov/2018021938

First US Edition 2018
Printed in the USA
Interior design by Jakob Vala

www.tinhouse.com

For Mom

CONTENTS

*Yet the Lord set his affection on your ancestors and loved them,
and he chose you, their descendants, above all the nations.*

DEUTERONOMY 10:15

Bone Thugs–N–Harmony.
Too much harmony. Not enough bone.

FRANK

When U-God from Wu-Tang said, *You ain't heard
us in a minute*, rap spoke straight to God.

When I broke bread, it was a syrup sandwich.
I licked all the body off my nails.

I saw two birds stalking a basketball court,
rivaling a confirmation when they spotted

buckled asphalt and saw a growing squall
go smooth. And when they dove to break the surface—

a reconciliation. I said to God, Just watch
the demonstration every night. You'll see

blackness kept in its station. I saw peace,
one time, in fuchsia dusk—a fair tomorrow.

And I saw dusk that plagiarized my one
and only prayer—

Hallelujah. I'm ready
to go searching for that mysterious dark
when nightfall proves to be empty before
the heavens turn red from the fire.

When God gave Ten Commandments—thou
shalt not do any work; must keep
it holy; honor father, mother;
never covet wife nor ox nor ass—

I heard *do work, daughter, wife,*   *his ass off.*

Mary said, *I deserve a steed for this. The sex
that didn't need bodies. This swag. No hip
craned nearly out its socket. Not one flex.*

Seduction

                *is when I'm on my knees. My lip
                gets licked by Common Whitlow.   You gotta get
                real comfortable, get both your hands dirty
                when thunderstorms play rough with wind. Just let
                it kiss you.*

                        I was only half of thirty
*when my body had its way with me. Much less
violent than you would think.   A kind of shame.
But what is change?*

Was I branded a new
woman? Was I a woman yet? I chew
myrrh now to soothe my throat. Feeding, I press
my chest against his mouth and say my name.

My church camp counselors said *fucking go*
to bed [no names], but they'd just taught us one
more Christian song—

> It only takes a spark
> to get a fire going—

> > > and we sang

loud as we could. Took in a lobbing pitch
of air. A held-out note. Vibrato good
enough for all the coming grab-ass, good
over-the-shirt action.

> > I left to go

find that one counselor awake, the one
with weed, listening to Snoop, instructing, *Spark*
that fat-ass J. God—

> by the way he sang

the J's long *a*, this guy was hot damn pitch
perfect. Gangsta. He swallowed all the pitch
of the Patuxent night. Made dark look good.

I loved him. *Yeah,* I told him, *boy, let's go*
do this. I took him in the woods. For one
second the moon opened its eye—a spark—
and closed it.

3

Then he told me he once sang
himself off a bluff. He ordered, *Sang, girl, sang,*
instead of *sing.*

Minus a howling pitch,
the wind is only timbre.

Yo, you good?

he said. Me—all swagger and time to go
talk up the story I'd become. The one
who saw the man in the moon hung like a spark
refusing expiration with each spark
of expectations.

Yeah, he did say sang,
I told the girls, when all I did was pitch
myself down in the dirt until all good
and dirty. No story. Just girl. No go.

The fire still went on. And then that one
boy fell right in, a fall leaving just one
hole burned in his windbreaker's sleeve, the spark
of his embarrassment. The crickets sang,
of course. The lanterns crackled. Light and pitch.
The sounds were unpredictable and good
as we expected. Echoes came to go.

Then the pitch of my skin sang at a vagrant spark
lighting up one spot on my thigh. A good
scar. I can go a week and not touch it.

But when I do, it's like my finger's not
fit for feeling. Like everything's too hot.

Like when you move over a boiling pot
and put your hand on the eye, waiting, and it ought
to burn.

       I bet Mary Magdalene, devout
down on her knees, had a thing for her hot palms
on someone else's tepid feet: the grip,
grit in her nails. The murky basin—alms
for sun-cracked cuticles. A hangnail's clip.

I saw a Bible, on a pedestal
to hold its weight, closing.   I heard its sighs.
A new martyr to canonize.   Too full,

I left my finger in it, felt the rise
I get when guys say, *Break me off a piece
of that.*

When fractured, I can tense, release,
and relax in slow-wave sleep with a fairy tale
where I knock out Sleeping Beauty, fucking cock
her on the jaw. She falls into the briar.
Pussy. I find her prince. I up and sock
him, too. I call each one of them a liar.

I damn the spindle's hundred years of sleep
because I rarely sleep. I curse the birds
who took their heads from out beneath their heap
of wings. When lovers look, they need no words.

And when a hound comes running after me,
a redbone with a smile baring its teeth
so white, I wake up with the majesty
of princesses who lie there underneath
a spell of something better still to come.

My eyes are blurry, my mouth dry and dumb.

I wish I'd dream a Lady Jesus exists,
insisting in the garden's olive trees,

I, too, can come and go from this.
I'll leave you in Gethsemane's
xystus, the beck and call of the cock,
and falling wind that always ends
on Hush. Go on. Do it. Deny
me, Peter.

        I'm a maenad shape-
shifting inside a sheltered cave.

And when the grave sky's body-farm
of gods and gutted animals
serves me, you'll eat me, masticate
me with your tongue. My mouth, a bit
of gristle.

        When I asked for grace
the dust hid all the stars, and not
a single thing happened. But now
I am the dust. The rivers choke
on my fine silt. The loess is
my body. All the fertile air
the firmament of my thick skin.

And then the Holy Spirit finds its voice.

This is me disillusioned with the mouth.
This is me thinking of the time I came
as fire in an apostle's throat. This is
me as the burn that a believer breathes.

This is me sucking on small stacks of dimes
tucked into either side of my frenulum.
This is my fissured tongue as wishing well.

I deserve no need for this. I call the space
between my lips my hunt for satisfaction.

I seek God.

He asks, as he asked Job, *Can you*
loosen Orion's belt?
I say, *Can* you?

I got everything I need in Virgo.

Her vertices accommodate my knees
when I hyperextend in her. I broke
a tibia once because my muscles seize
at night, nothing to do to ease the choke
of too-excited nerves except to curve
your toes and let it happen

                just as a star
                happens when it's done hiding in the swerve
                of dissipating clouds. The charges spar.

I like it. At lightning's eleventh hour,
I be like, Damn, Virgo. Is this your jam?
Making your skirt look better than a bower,
your stomach's kind of parallelogram.

The sky is not a dome. There is no shelter.

I be like, Teach me what it's like to burn
in all the vapors, how to never swelter
so hot my core turns into iron's churn
and boil. Show me where you hide your blood.

One time I told someone I saw the Big
Dipper, but didn't. Boötes and cud,
but didn't. Sagitta was in a twig.

I know the bodies of the body well.

> For just as Jonah was three days, three nights
> in the belly of the fish, so will the Son
> of Man be three days and three nights in the heart
> of the earth.

Elect won't always equal worth.
I've spent days in my belly, nights in my heart.

For some, it don't mean a thing without the swing
of a gavel, and a trace of doubt can trump
a circumstance.

Oh beautiful for skies
too small.

Today, the paper boasted this—
Five Local Policemen Tied to KKK—
italicized as if to shout, *It's new.*
This.

When I went outside, thinking I knew
something of Frost's birches, that endless swing
of left to right, the day managed to trump
up stillness.
        Today, I'm reading noon. The sky's
pastoral. Cumuli passing for this
creature or that one, stallions, maybe K-
9 dogs, maybe the alphabet with K
then O, maybe this sentence: *That kid knew*
he had no business here.

                I spot the swing,
far off, of scales. The winning suit and trump
card in a game of spades.

                Today, the skies
are angled sides in the A-frame of this
old house we built and then forgot. There's this
rafter, rotting, sort of looking okay;
but, later, it ages to wood all new
and gnarled. Every knot a knee. The swing
of a young girl's legs.

Today I told Donald Trump
the story of a woman. How the skies
came out of her wherever. Spacious skies.
Dark skies. Grown woman skies. Coalsack at this
time of the month spreads deep. That kind of K
you see in Crux, that's her. The bloody new
moon, her. Yessir, you're going to have to swing
a huge dick if you're going to hit it.

                    Trump
came out of *triumph*. Trump (verb): play a trump
on; win a trick.

          Tonight, I'm running skies
through my sewing machine, connecting this
evening to morning, hand stitching a K
for force. It isn't dark enough. My new
windows need blackout shades.

                    Tonight, the swing
of things. Tonight, okay, if any world
were new. Ever. If swinging skies were spume
preserved in amber. If Trump.
                    If even this—

at a bar, a man says, *Love the hair,* says it's
the best hair, baby.   *I'm Republican*
                    but would totally go liberal for you;

at a gas station, a man's *Damn girl, those tits*
knocks me into the pump and I, too, can
be machine. Shudder. Waiting for use. Tick.   Queue.

When I was young, in our basement, where Africa
hung on the wall, my parents danced to Isaac Hayes's

Hot Buttered Soul. I insisted its real name,
Hot Monkey Love, was better. Lil' bit racist.

It happens. So I tell myself.

                    One time, Dad tried
to race a smoke on the side of the house he thought
we couldn't see, maybe hoping the wind
would wash off the smell of a cop's night shift, maybe
refill the sockets of his knocked-out teeth.

That's when I realized that breath was white.

Get it right, Jesus. Get you a gun.
This is your chance at vigilante.

Bring this shit home and fucking ante
up your omnipresence. Because
in the beginning, there was
it good?

        It's not. Where is your free-
for-all? What of that jealousy?

This is your chance to be a man
who keeps the shells because he can;
and, when he shoots, he always cocks
his head up toward his shadow box
shiny with carbon-copied gods
and gutted animals.   Thy rod's
useless.   The good word   cannot make
morning beget another take
on mourning.

Say you've been abused,
white man's burden, and can't get used
to it.
No need to shake. You're stable.
Your hands wash clean in the water table.

Or,   bless us, Lord, to these
electrons, nuclei, our bonds
between the charge that corresponds
to charges.

Dear Lord, please
bless all the girth of black
Mandingo-looking Hercules,
cracked-out preemies, the ashy knees,
negroes yakety-yak
articulate.

Bless this
matter. Black life, apparently,
now matters. Saw the effigy
on FB.

Matter: criss-
cross bandage on a wound.

Matter: of substance.

First dead man
I saw? My grandfather deadpan
in his casket, more pruned
than ever, face shaved clean.

My mother said he used to call
all white men Mr. Charlie. *All
'nem*, she says. She says he'd lean
and never sweep the rooms
he and my grandma cleaned at night
at Michigan State where all the white
chalk was a blizzard's blooms
in Mom's eyes. *He would say,
Mr. Charlie ain't shit.* Now Grandma can't
remember it.

Matter: a slant.

Say of the matter, Say
it ain't so.   Matter: state.

When Baltimore blew up in May
after the police killed Freddie Gray,
my brother got irate
at News 13: *It's one*
damn neighborhood. Whole town's not up
in smoke. I told him, *Frank,* *get up,*
grab your TV and gun
it down your block and see
what happens.

                                                              Matter: consequence:

if then after before and hence:
matter of fact: you, me.

For that matter, were we
pretty back when we first begun
in God's image? When is it done?

How sweet the sound of free.

The dark matter accounts
for all the space in space.

                        I saw
a dead man in the moon, the maw
of a hagfish, an ounce
of lymph.

18

                              Matter: no matter

but for breath, its water in the air
fogging my glasses when, in prayer
this morning, the grackles' chatter
distracts me, and it's how
perfect an omen: a blackbird, ants
on its body so it has a chance
to survive, at least, for now.

My spirit animal, at least, for now.

The gospel says that flesh gives birth
to flesh and it gives birth to spirit.

So many pregnancies though it
can't possibly efface to a state
more open.

              What the dove it was
once had were sacs and hollow bones
for air.

              Somewhere, there are black ghost
knife fish bearing a charging current,
and flukes, no body cavity.

If you have no body, can you
be filled? They egest waste without
a taste of what it's like to pace
the tannic mouthfeel of a moan.

I dream fishermen
offer chum, instead of loaves,
to catch my hunger.

                    I eat my body.
                    I barely even dry heave.
                    ___ _____ ___ berry, the sweeter ___ _____.

What's sweeter than a paramour who's kept
and loving it: the way we say a man
keeps a mistress instead of has a mistress
because *keep* means possession, hold, and grip?

Bad bitch.

            She loves that he left in a serein
tonight—fine rain and not a single cloud—
that the lightbulb in the lamp beside
her bed is dying, that it buzzes as
an insect does, the flashing filament
the thorax, shell the exoskeleton.

She loves the dog that's hollering outside,
how it could be where he stood earlier,
next to a bird that must've hit the ground
like a bare back door—such aimless force, its head
sits perpendicular to its broad chest.

The dog must have its hungry face in it.

She loves thinking what it'd be like to bark
and grumble in your throat, to make a sound
of such alarm for both pleasure and pain
that people stand back. She hopes to make a noise
next time he comes over, an afternoon
on a day that's warm enough for open windows,

when somebody will hear her, stop, and think
a mother tongue of glossolalia.

                The devil got up in me something fierce.

See, I have a thing for dead white guys.
Right now, Robert Herrick.

              Love me
Hesperides, the ending's guise
of a start—
            goddess Electra's come-
to-tears moment birthing a sea
of flowers.

I can die the death
of poets. Caesura in my breath
on someone's uvula. Esprit
vibrations. Resonator.

I used
to say fecund like begun, refused
correction.

Then somebody told
me my body's not mine to hold.

To hold—grasp, carry, or support,
detain, incarcerate, intern,
impound; the what after the court;
archaic: *Girl, you got to learn
your place.* Adhere; maintain.

Let's ball,
white boy. Next time I get *exotic*, I'll call
you Hoss. Third person. You're beside yourself.

Instead of *You can get it*, Hoss *can get it.*

When Hoss is getting it, he describes, at length,
the horny femur of a rooster's leg
good for cockfights because, of course, Hoss knows
about roosters and cockfights.

              When Hoss asks
if it's racist to call him Hoss, *No sir.*
Got white-guy friends. Fuckloads of Allman Brothers.

Me: You're a hassa, asking me that. And Hoss:

Hassa?

        Then me: Hassa: as in Pacino
as in "pig" as in a crooked cop as in
Scarface. Hoss hasn't seen *Scarface.*

                     Perfect.

Shadows from opened blinds cross Hoss's neck.
Some kind of Jesus, though I'm never saved.

I put my makeup on and make
my face in shades blending to shadow.

A man looked good because I'd not
seen him before.
             Fuck yes I pulled
a woman's belt loop just to get
closer. I was low enough to touch
somebody's *This is me.*

I've known
the darker the juice, the warmer the slur
of spit, acid, bile, and gut.

Some fifty times I've read Milton—
the pandemonium of dogs
crazy in love with born again,
chewing their way back in that beast
of a woman. Maybe sixty times.

I didn't read the guy in the club
who pushed up on me, see the crowd
circling around to watch him grab
my thigh and break my strap. Off rhythm.
A hand in every -ism. Such
exoticism in the dark.

Circumlocution—

        what is fault
        if not a deed, done did, amiss?

Solution—

        friend who took me home
        and *Yo, you know that guy was just*
        a racist troglodyte.

           I looked
up *troglodyte* and teased my hair
so high it cleared the mirror, cracked
five teeth right out the wide-toothed comb.

I put my makeup on and broke
my face into a hundred pigments.
Some of the hues red as the part
of the mouth nobody ever sees.

John had a revelation, said he saw
a new heaven and earth. The first ones passed
away. This time there was no single sea.

I read the same verses. I saw the *no.*

I wrote a love poem to white
guys after learning hair
is just dead skin:

          I want to pin
you down and brush against your chest.
You say, *Damn, girl, your dermis is so
pretty.* You say burn all do-rags.
You say grow it out. Go natural.

This is the moment when we refurbish ourselves.
Rising and falling, dust and dander, mites.
We need a black light and a microscope.
I want to see you shed. I want your sheath.

I wrote another after learning
orgasm comes from the Greek *orgasmós*
from organ, like *swoll' up*—wrote, yes,

God bless my sense of this is our
body—that intersection—fucked
and fucker, gutted, gut. Boy, let
me get that subjectivity

again. My legs around your back
so you can carry me. I don't
know if this means acceptance, though,
if I'm the part of us that dangles.

In bed, we'll read *The Marriage of Heaven and Hell*

together, like it's some duet or two-
man play. You do your Milton voice that sounds

like Heston's Moses, and you say Blake sounds
like that. I wax falsetto, using two

half notes: Genius, Harvest, Folly, Lions.
I claim the mouth of water, you the brick

brothel. We settle into Hell's big brick
house typeset in its chambers: eagles, lions.

You get the vipers and the dragon-man.
We both get the desire, cloud, and fire.

When we've both had enough Maker's to fire
kindling with our mouths, I say, Pretend we're man

and wife, pretend we live together in
my Eden Avenue apartment here

in Cincinnati. Say we're growing old here.

I'm Blake's Raven and you are dawning in

the red wheat hardened in the fields. When, all
of a sudden, you aren't smart enough to read

another section; your pale face is all
covers. I turn the light off, squint to read

the frost's small cuts on the bare window's page,
thinking of how *luciferous* means light,

how dawn should beg forgiveness with the light
on its back.
                    Dawn, an apologetic page.

New-powder snow fills the rim of angels.
I wonder when the weatherman will say

it'll melt, when you'll wake up, and whether I'll say,
You won't believe what happened to the angels.

They never speak the language of the body.

I have a dream I corner Gabriel and tell
him how, one time, I cored the moon and lived,
for a month of Sundays, warm inside its curve.

He whispers, *Never tell*, then tells me how
he holds dearest the best part of "Hail Mary,"
the Tupac song. He raps for me—*Revenge,*
next to getting pussy, is like the sweetest joy.

I tell him about evening and morning good.
He tells me of Eve's leaves after the fall's
exposure.

He reminds me of the verse
"Let everything that hath breath praise the Lord."

Hold it, he says. *A few seconds at least*—

but my crooked teeth are weary of their sockets.
They're falling out in mounds as if my mouth
has held a hundred mouths. My hoodie's pockets
can't hold them all. Tomorrow, they'll go south

in padded envelopes addressed to no
one at nowhere, enough Forever stamps
to take them there and back—because I know
there's nothing to a molar's bite, no clamps

tight in the jaw to chew something to raw
again—blood line, gristle, mouth spent—to spit
aside to save something to savor. I saw
a gullet so voracious it could fit

a *How did it…?* and all the gist of   *Where?*
a woman lost too much of her to bare
in the middle of the mourning.

                              Martha bared
herself to Mary,   *Love? Give me exodus.*
The leaving.

        As we're praising Lazarus,
you cry while I think, next to this,
the exequy, there's nothing like the fuss
the body makes over itself.

Mmm. Rigor.
Liquids expelled and firm muscles, the bone
the only lasting truth that can't transfigure
itself to something worse or better.

I've thrown
a stone into a brook to break my face.
I've scratched my skin to know just how it felt—
attacked by your own person. Kissed the pelt
of a sheep sick with blackleg.

There is space

when empty caves become the bodies' tombs.
Space for going. That flight the air exhumes.

When Jeezy said   that Jesus said   the sky's
our only limit, rap asked God who deferred
it to the dirt interred around the incus,
the anvil of the ear's middle passage.

The body of us.
Never the heartbeat we've heard.
The breath before *don't*.

Macon, GA. Miss Ellen Craft. The daughter
of a slave and her white master—i.e., slaughter.

Looks white enough to dress up like a white
man—i.e., sacrifice—and start the flight,
her dark-skinned husband playing her valet.
He's dark enough, convincing in the way
he says *Missus.*

                    I wonder how the pants
felt on her thighs and if she had the chance

to clench a kegel.   Or, did she say, *Way
so soft?* And know that soft can calcify?

We have a chance to rectify,
Black women.
                    Find your American Girl.
Kirsten. Bind her with butcher's twine.

It's her fault all black dolls were ugly.

You wished your hair would fall like that.

Now put her in the trunk and sit
on it. Light up a grape Swisher.

Swing by the Metro Mart to get
some Chester's fried chicken and ask
the guy, *Yo, where the 40s at?*
so he can tell you how the law
won't give you more than 32
and you say, *Well, fuck the man.*

Today you're feeling petulant
and someone catcalled you with *Girl,*
you got some fat steak when your ass
is grown, and he was black and that's
as bad as when the white guy thought
it fine to say he likes it native.

Feel sated. Lean back. Always ride
dirty. Say, *Officer, I'm sorry*
but I'm just going to have to play
it louder now. Go on and claim
your stake. If you want harder, you
should have to ask for it by name.

Be loud as Bathsheba's song of Solomon.

Her verses' husky bit of tenor. Range
we usually ascribe to men.

                          Verse one—
I knew David was watching me.   Some strange.
I wanted it.

Verse two—*I'm testament*
to a woman real down to follow her gut
instinct for do-me.   I will not repent.

Say Queen of Israel. Sang it, even.   *But*
don't think, Damn, that woman straight lusts for fame.
Your recognition is too short a story
driven by apparitions.

                    My real name
means daughter of oath. It's like a mandatory
obligation to truth. But what if names lie?

What if I let my body testify
even after learning that some select
people can say *grab them by the pussy?*   I,
with my rights and privileges, there, undo and elect
to sew my labia closed, using a butterfly
loop and Pantone Black 7 thread. It's then
I'm most colored.
                    Bleeding.
                        Now the man who said,
You're black even down there, girl,   says, *Say when,*
woman.

I tell him I have never bled
the bright red of a finch;
                    but, often, I
assume the brown body of a cactus wren—
ass up, chest out. The strength enough to fly
through a closed door. Just bust inside where ten
flowers, evolvulus, are screwed, each hit
with a merciless sun.   But they don't wilt.

                                        They will

their way through thirsty—thin bodies unfit
for death like a black woman standing, still.

(Still: up to and including now or time
mentioned; it's all the same; nevertheless;
something like how my name will always rhyme
with America, oppress matching regress.)

Slaughterhouse says, *Moving on . . .*

                              and rap remembers

its recurring dream—the swim to Africa
where disembodied voices yell, *There's no
room for a hiraeth in your bones.* But in
marrow, there's substance, healing, narrow passage.

I walk through civilizations
of fire ants. No lamentations.
I am environment and genotype.

The southern cricket's getting hype
while Ephesians says, *Be completely humble.*

I'd like to say I've seen a humble spark
not fizzle out or fuel a fire. Just
maintain within the limits of its burn.

I'd like to say I've seen a humble spark
turn into wood itself—deciduous.
Maintain within the limits of its burn
and never turn to ash. And maybe not
turn into wood itself.

             Deciduous
milk teeth of children shed after a time
and never turn to ash and maybe not.

This time, don't brush the fire off your shoulder.

Milk teeth of children shed after a time
of death. The gums drained of their blood. Feel it
this time. Don't brush the fire off your shoulder.
Feel the burn of a baby's bite on toughened nipples.

Apostle John saw the sun burn to a black
dark as sackcloth made of hair. The moon was blood.

I'm covering my head, like Kool
G. Rap said, in this red zone. Dead.

This ain't no motherland, though **fek**-uhnd
as fuck.
       Florida's the only time
and place I've said, *It's a black thing,*
you wouldn't understand,   like I
will never understand the love-
bugs fucking ass to ass,   or man
standing his ground, shotgun in hand,
shooting at cans like they're an unkindness
of ravens.

       Seven years I have
mothered this nature into a woman.
The moon, her crevices, a tree
the sharpness of her tough skin split.

Eve knew she didn't need a man to be
a mother. Didn't need his rib/God's hand
to be made. She was already every sea.
A month of Sundays. And the singeing brand
scarring the sky. Woman. The W.
Cassiopeia.

       She said, *I preceded you,*
Adam. You didn't have to fracture you,
break frame to find me.

True, I let you do
the work, putting in work. Sure. Own this land.
I am the ground and its fertility.

Now toil this: Yessir, you've been unmanned.

Call this in the beginning's constancy
where there ain't nothing but the cold and hollow
space of your chest.

                    I'm tidal. Taste me. Swallow.

I, myself, put a rock between my legs
as if I'd birthed it or fucked it dry.

Now I'm gonna let my nuts hang, Lord.

Between my legs, the eve of day's
coming darkness stained with a word
sounding something like a destination—

When did we get to nigger? Just
how far is it to nigger?

                    Here.

I tell Lil' Kim that nothing makes
this woman feel better than telling God,
See my slow goddess and my two
fists, same size as my beating heart.
Same fists, the size of my stomach.

Bleek says you sick with that fetish, that gotta eat,
and rap schools God and sustenance and hunt.

The air is waterlogged. Niggas ain't thirsty.

Bitch, please calls out an orison for mercy.

Black mama's castor oil, no revival.

Rap says niggas ain't hungry anymore.

On an X-ray, the stomach's curve is more like
a waxing moon than organ, just a phase
unchanging in the belly's sort-of womb.

When I was young at church camp, we would get out
the Ouija board and try to levitate,
smashing a flashlight in one cheek to make
a ghost story turn horror. I would make-
believe spirituality.
                          Things like
possession—
                 going through a "knowing" phase
like all believers do—blessing to womb
to tomb. *Growing.*

Tonight, I'm playing out
"Go Down, Moses" as if it'll levitate
right off the turntable. Or levitate
higher, a disc remixing the sky.

                           To make
the sky move would be sick,   or really, like,
anything.   Maybe time could be a phase.

I press a flashlight hard against my womb,
spreading my legs to see if white comes out.

If only anything came slightly out
of the ordinary, my skin would levitate,
each layer would hover.   I aspire to make

a glory of a woman rising like
a field below a bluff, but not a phase
of failed perception. An evening.

                             There's womb
in my throat now.

                     One time I heard the womb
of a woman's voice when I was high and out
with a Nas and Marley track to levitate
over a k hole. Whole hook seemed to make
sense when it called for *Somebody*. I'm like,
Yeah. Somebody.

Nobody. Will I phase
out sense when every mouth proves just a phase
then only jaw?

It was *Sabali*, from the womb
of a foreign tongue—Bambara. *Patience.* I'm out

of listening. Tonight will levitate
above my upper lip so I can't make
my face out separate from the dark. Make like
you saw me making love and crawling out
of the dirt. You saw my sex straight levitate
off my body like this is a phase—grounded—

and I'm turning

to fly with Lilith, succuba,
(two winged Night Hag with all her prophecies
inside their pussies) right to Nineveh,
the female place-nation-debaucheries.

We get it.
                    There, dear Jezebel can swear
by some new Baal. And sick and tired Eve
says, *Damn,*
            I could have been the rightful heir
to fuck forgiveness, snake a fresh ink-sleeve
or tourniquet.

It won't ever get old,
Lilith says, *being the moody sex. They don't*
want us hysterical or loud or bold
but like the way they reek of us and won't
wash off our sour. It will only take
a spark to help us taint the night awake.

When Lauryn Hill found
her manifest destiny
in Gore-Tex and sweats,

I told God that's all
the heat we need. August haze.
A huge graffiti

Jesus prays on brick.
There's *Domino, nigga.* There's
Rose for the lady.

I breathe *Hallelujah*'s feminine endings.

Tonight's not offering its arm
but a place for me inside its hoodie.

I will not wear *Americoon,*
the blacks, the go-to Halloween
costume for Ivy Leaguers, beleaguered
Bluegum.   5-0,
                    we see you. White
                    House, we see you.

                                    That place will turn
to just a storefront, GOLD n GUNS.

A perfect certainty—a storm won't clean
my sweating skin and all the rain can't muffle
the *What motherfucker What That's what*
I thought Goddamn.

                    I can do all things
through ~~Christ which strengtheneth~~ me.

John saw
the dead
standing
before
God's throne.

I see the exodus of light.

Let there
be black never absorbing white. Let there
be skin born back on every scar and tear.

Let there be no oceans or weapon-wear
of tides raking the shores.   Sister, stand there.

I see the exodus of light.

Let there
be not afraid, for you are with the fair
and mighty god of your body.   Stare.

Be skin born back on every scar, and tear
that undershirt, brother. Let us all bare
our weight. Let there be loose. And then, let there.

I see the exodus of light let there
be evening with no mourning.

Say the prayer
of your own name at dawn and echo *Where?*

Be skin born back on every scar and tear,
a voice no longer trembling, *Why?*   the air
drying the eyes closing on *Who?*   Aware.

I see the exodus of light.

                  Let there
be skin born back on every scar and tear.

Hold it, the angel Gabriel said.

In my kitchen. Those flowers. They're called
Blue My Mind. Sometimes I wear the petals.

Outside, a dark and empty heaven.

A wind gone on about its blackness.

ACKNOWLEDGMENTS

I am incredibly grateful to everyone who has supported this book for so long.

Forever thanks to Jeff Parker.

Thanks to my UTMFA family, especially Lynne Bartis.

Thanks to Scott, Caroline, Brendan, Laura, Jane, my docking crew, and all the Disquieters.

Thanks to my boys, David Reamer and Dan Dooghan, for pulling me out of the cave. All we do is win.

Thanks to Shane Hinton for being Shane Hinton.

Special thanks to my girls, Juliana Gray and Sarah Fryett, for things we don't talk about in public.

Special thanks to the artists and apostles who, in one way or another, made cameos in this book: U-God and Method Man ("Wu-Tang"); Matthew the Apostle (Matthew 20:40); Tupac

("Hail Mary"); Young Jeezy ("Hypnotize"); Slaughterhouse ("Move On"); Kool G. Rap and D.J. Polo ("Home Sweet Home"); Lil' Kim ("No Time"); Jay-Z, Memphis Bleek, and Beanie Sigel ("1-900-Hustler"); Nas and Damian Marley ("Patience"); The Fugees ("Ready or Not"); and Paul the Apostle ("Philippians 4:13").

Endless thanks to Rob Spillman, Tony Perez, Matthew Dickman, Jakob Vala, Sabrina Wise, Jessica Roeder, and the entire team at Tin House for this chance to say the things I need to say, and for all their hard work.

Megan, thank you a trillion times over.

All my love and gratitude to my family: Dad, Frank, Mandy, and Frankie.

This one's for you, Mom. You're a true survivor. You're my hero.